The Ultimate Guide on Cryptocurrency

Cryptocurrency

by Neo Monefa

Table of Contents

1. Introduction

Cryptocurrency, or the electronically created line of codes of monetary value, or simply put, digital currency can be defined as a medium of exchange just like the usual currencies such as USD. However, what makes them different from the conventional currencies is that they are designed to exchange digital information by using the principles of cryptography. This cryptography controls the security of transactions as well as the mining of new coins.

The technology that will have the greatest impact on the world economy and its future is block chain technology. Yes, you read it correctly. It is not artificial intelligence, solar energy or even self-driving car. The first wave of the digital revolution got us the Internet that was full of information. **READ ON.**

2. What is Bitcoin?

Currencies have had a long history on this planet and their fortunes quite literally rise and fall with the times that we live in. In addition, the latest in this long line to rise to prominence is that of the ever amazing and the extraordinarily cryptic crypto currency of Bitcoin. This brand new form of online currency which was introduced by its mysterious creator Satoshi Nakamoto in 2008, finally came tumbling out of the currency closet a year later and since its grand introduction, this piece of digital moo-la has been burning a hole in digital wallets ever since.

Bitcoin with its unheard of rapid advancement to the top of the digital currency food chain has surprised everyone, what was once just a past time and novelty of bored techies and cyber geeks is now a household word. Just the word "Bitcoin" ushers in many different thoughts and images. There is both the controversy and the triumph of this new mode of transaction.

Something akin to when the first credit cards came out or even the creation of the internet, the introduction of this sleek and efficient digital piece of commerce is nothing less than world changing. Whether you agree with it or not, like it or dislike, if you have been paying attention to its progress it can't be denied that the ascendancy of Bitcoin is nothing short of remarkable. And what this currency consists of and what it is not backed up with has made it an altogether unique phenomenon all to itself.

Bitcoin is a decentralized digital currency, which means that it can be stored and used anywhere without a centralized control of its supply. Every other currency in world circulation is backed up, one way or another, to a national currency. But Bitcoin is free of all that, it is not locked down to the whims of local inflation or the edicts of congress and parliament. Bitcoins are simply worth whatever it is that they are exchanged for. There is nothing else quite like it.

The decentralized nature of Bitcoin is something akin to a precious metal like gold. Gold is a decentralized currency that always has the same value. You dig up a piece of Gold in a mine and it is considered exactly the same as a gold bar lying around at a Fort Knox gold reserve, it doesn't change. But unlike bitcoins, gold is not digital and that same gold bar from Fort Knox would not do much good for you when making a purchase on Amazon, you can't send a solid bar of gold through your computer screen.

Believe me I tried it! I got a gold bar stuck in an old Gateway computer monitor back in 1999 trying to buy a Ricky Martin CD! If only I had bitcoins! Just kidding, of course! Just a little bit of humor to illustrate my point and break up the monotony! But in all seriousness, this is what is so incredible about bitcoins, they have the stand alone property of a precious metal like gold yet they ARE digital, and you CAN send them through your computer, cell phone or any other digital relaying device and buy that Ricky Martin CD or whatever else it is you want!

This is where Bitcoin has the best of both worlds; it is just as decentralized as gold but digital. Which of course has lent Bitcoin the self-explanatory nickname of, "digital gold", and as Bitcoin's profits and prospect soar it continues to be that proverbial and literal gold mine for its patrons as they mine and pine their lives away for this digital super currency.

Introduced by a creator who elected to remain anonymous, the inventor of this currency may remain a bit of a mystery but the applications of how to use it are not. Using Bitcoin does not require a banker or some other savvy administrative official it is so easy and straightforward that anyone can use it, anyone can store it, and amazingly, just about anyone can mint this form of digital currency. There are absolutely no middle men involved in the process; no bank is needed and there are no transaction fees. With this currency no one even needs to know your name, since all transactions can be carried out completely anonymous. There is a public log of activities and the transactions themselves are recorded in the public ledger but the name of the person who is using Bitcoin is not made known. This creates quite a revolution when it comes to currency and privacy.

While this pseudo anonymous nature of the public ledger has been criticized as aiding cyber criminals, it has in reality prevented much cyber-crime in the way of identity theft since users can rest assured that they don't have to put any blatantly identifiable information they don't have to worry about anyone stealing. And as we will discuss in later chapters of this book, there is a way we can still trace the transaction histories of crooks if need be, so really the public log only helps those that it is meant to; the honest and law abiding consumer.

The public log that user activity is recorded into is known as the "block chain" The public log is referred to as this because all information is recorded in chunks or "blocks" of information that are tied (chained) together. This activity that lies stored in this block chain is not processed by any administrative official it is computed directly by a vast network of communicating nodes that are running the Bitcoin software. As the name implies a block (new group of accepted transactions) spirals out in a chain from every transaction. Approximately every ten minutes transactions are bundled into a block and added to a block chain.

Once a block is created and added to the chain it is then published to all nodes allowing the software to record what amount of Bitcoin has been spent in each transaction, preventing any possible double charge or discrepancy. A copy is also automatically stored in what is known as a "digital wallet", a collection of addresses and "private keys" owned by one person. This wallet is a program that exists in the cloud or in the computers of Bitcoin "miners" who participate in adding collected transactions to the block chain.

The "private key" is your PIN number when using Bitcoin; this is used, coupled with your account number which is the "public key". It is after this verification of the private key to the public key that the funds are released. The private key consists of a long sequence of letters and numbers and it usually begins with the number "five". This series of numbers and letters in the private key is matched up with your Bitcoin address (public key) and your bitcoins are then unlocked at that address.

Working just like an e-mail address but used just for the receipt of the Bitcoin itself, you can send money through Bitcoin to any email address or Bitcoin wallet address. Working on a "peer to peer" network to verify and authorize the transactions that are performed. With no reliance on any government, bank or organization these digital coins rely on cryptographic protocols and a network of every day normal people to store, mint and transfer these funds.

Bitcoin is quite a revolution in convenience and personal freedom. Bitcoins are easily transferable and can even be transferred from phone to phone through mobile applications. The simplistic nature of how Bitcoin works allows you to cut out any middlemen or any other every day stressors of maintaining normal bank accounts. With Bitcoin if you have a mobile phone in your pocket, then you essentially have a bank in your pocket as well. It's that easy. Just download the application and you can control your currency.

3. What are Altcoins?

A virtual currency has been defined as "a type of unregulated, digital money, which is issued and usually controlled by its developers, and used and accepted among the members of a specific virtual community".

Whilst the US Department of Treasury defined it as "a medium of exchange that operates like a currency in some environments, but does not have all the attributes of real currency".

It has also been said that cryptocurrencies do not have the status as legal tender.

But who decides what legal tender is?

We can look at cryptocurrency as an alternative to the age-old barter system where it is up to the individual as to what to barter and in this case millions of people are choosing to barter *trade in cryptocurrency* Altcoins.

If we look at cryptocurrency or Altcoins as not being legal tender then how has bitcoin soared from $1 per coin to over $1300 per coin. That means there are a lot of people who agree with each other that it is their own personal legal tender, but not the government's legal tender.

It appears that living off the financial grid is now a reality. No charges, no fees, no interest, no middlemen.

And why would the government, banks and financial institutions consider Altcoins as legal tender when they have no way of getting their sticky little fingers on your piece of pie.

The banks and financial institutions must be fuming. At the time of writing Bitcoin alone traded $469,489,000 over the past 24 hours.

Here is the latest on how much the top 10 altcoins traded in the past 24 hours in US Dollars (at time of publication):

1 Bitcoin $469,489,000
2 Ethereum $307,526,000
3 Ripple $41,699,800
4 Litecoin $35,321,100
5 Dash $20,910,100
6 Ethereum Classic $88,663,400

7 NEM NEM $6,797,300
8 Monero $10,839,300
9 Augur Augur $4,844,940
10 Golem $21,641,700

These are serious numbers….and the new financial reality.

Remembering that this is only the top 10 out of hundreds of different Cryptocurrencies.

4. Top Cryptocurrency Exchanges

Essentially there are three ways to transfer bitcoins; through middle men, currency exchanges, and person to person transactions. Just like through the traditional banking model. When you conduct your bitcoin business through the use of middle men or as they are

known, "Bitcoin Exchange Intermediaries", you are using a highly knowledgeable third party that handles all of the more complex technicalities of the exchange.

In exchange for their customer service and knowledgebase you will most likely be charged a fee for their services, these fees usually run anywhere from 1 to 10 percent. This may cut into your overall bitcoins but will save you a bad headache in the end since all of the technical aspects of the exchange will be placed on their shoulders and not yours.

If you are worried about paying a sizable fee one way to circumvent this is to utilize a "Bitcoin Exchange". These exchanges work to directly connect people who are buying and selling their bitcoins. Although you avoid a fee this way, the downside is that all of those complicated technicalities that you would have been shielded from when using a middle man type service are in the forefront for you to figure out!

For this reason using a Bitcoin Exchange can be somewhat intimidating to a fresh bitcoin user. It is precisely due to the fact that you deal with all of this on your own that exchanges cut the price so significantly. So if you can deal with some of the headache of managing this stuff on your own this is the way to go, but if you need a little extra help you would most likely be better off just paying the fee to have a middle man do the work for you.

Currently the most popular Bitcoin Exchange platform out there is that of "Coinbase". Operating out of the United States, Coinbase has users sign up for their service online. To create an account with them all you have to do is create a user name and a password. After this

Coinbase will send a confirmation to your e-mail address and you are good to go.

Now you can start buying some bitcoins, just log into Coinbase and select the amount of bitcoins that you want and then click on "Buy Bitcoin". The funds will then be transferred out of your bank account and in just a few days after purchase your money will then resurface as bitcoins. You will then receive an e-mail to notify you that your bitcoins have been placed inside of your Coinbase wallet.

If you are primarily using your smart phone to conduct transactions with Coinbase you can set up a "Two Factor Identification" system.

The best way to do this is to download an app on your phone that will handle all of the security features and other essential protocol for the transactions that you will be conducting.

Basically what this method does is that it marks your phone, identifying it by phone number, proving that this phone is indeed associated with your account. With this established all you need is a coinbase password and your smart phone and you are ready to conduct transactions.

To make this process even easier Coinbase has the novelty (and the good business sense) to have their very own app called, "Authy" available for download from the Google Plat store. After installing this app all you have to do is enter your phone number and verify your e-mail address and then you can log into Coinbase, link up your phone and then ready to transfer some bitcoins!

If you aren't too sure about using a third party wallet however, I would recommend taking the bitcoins out as soon as possible and putting them in your own self-managed wallet. Taking the bitcoins into your own wallet will of course reduce your third party risk down to zero and when your absolute risk is down to zero percent those are certainly good odds. So I would recommend transferring into your own self-managed, personal wallet as soon as possible. With it working sort of in a combination of buying and trading; it's good to be able to use an efficient, verified and knowledgeable platform like Coinbase.

Along with using platforms that specifically specialize in bitcoins transfer it might also be a good idea to use a traditional "currency exchange". With a standard currency exchange you can simply deposit money in one currency and then trade that money in for your currency of choice; bitcoins. You can play with the numbers a bit with a currency exchange by offering to exchange the currency at any rate that you choose. This is a bartering process where you can raise your bid while the other party lowers their asking price until the two of you agree on a rate somewhere in the middle, always falling somewhere between the highest bid and the lowest asking price.

To get started with a currency exchange the first thing that you need to do is to set up an account that links to your banking information. After this is set up send over the amount of cash that you wish to use, to the currency exchange. After this you can place an order to have them transferred into bitcoins.

But before you make your transfer you will need to be aware that there are two types of transfer orders that can be made; that of "market orders" and "limit orders". With a market order you specify that you would like to have a transfer made as soon as possible at the best possible price that is available at the time. This can be beneficially if time is of the essence and you need bitcoins right away but you may not get the best exchange rate in the process.

If you have the time to getter a better deal though it is advisable to wait around on a limit order. With a limit order you can limit the exchange rate down to very specific parameters. With this option you can specify that you only wish to spend a certain amount of money and that you are willing to wait until someone emerges with that exact price. As long as you keep your specifications to a recent trade price you should be successful. I have personally known some people that have gotten some great deals this way, so come on and try it! As the new marketplace, the internet was made for Haggling, so just let them know your limit!

For all of these exchange platforms it is recommended that you develop and maintain a personal or business account to keep up with activity. Security is of course of vital importance no matter what system you use and you will also be required to show your personal identification when making these exchanges.

Besides these well-traveled third party routes to transfer your bitcoins, you can skip out on the third party all together and opt to the transferring of bitcoins by doing it on a "person to person" basis. This is done with real life people in your local area that you meet up with and conduct the exchange right there in person with them. This is the simplest of the techniques used for transfer but some believe this is the trend of the future as monetary establishments like Bitcoin move further and further away from centralization and into individual bitcoin exchange.

When transferring your bitcoins on the individual level it is always a good idea to know as much as you can about the person you are trading with. There are several local sites that you can use to get a better picture of the person before you make your transfer. Craigslist probably isn't the best choice but other sites such as LocalBitcoins.com are an excellent resource since they have multi-faceted rating systems that do a thorough check on the person's previous background and experience with bitcoins.

After first initiating your bitcoins transfer you need to make sure that you find a safe place to meet in person to conduct your trade. Always remember to keep safety your number one priority. No matter how good of a deal something may seem do not just go rushing in. First you need to plan out how and where you are going to do your Bitcoin trading, be sure to pick a place that is comfortable for both of you.

After all the other person may be just as leery about meeting you as you are of them. Like my mom used to say, "Everyone's a stranger until they meet!" that holds true with bitcoin trade as well. You are two completely different people bumping into each other, so you might as well be cordial and at least try to get minimally acquainted. This may be a big step for you, cut my number one advice when you meet up for a personal exchange of bitcoins is to just be calm and be yourself. Try not to worry to much and relax. I know this is most likely easier said than done, but it's the truth. Don't view it as a big deal or get to heavy about it because your unease could possibly set off alarm bells in your trading partners mind, after all he is just as suspicious of you and most likely scoping you out for any kind of social defect as well.

I remember one time when I was in college I met another student on campus to sell my I-pod and as soon as I saw this dude he was tweaking me out completely. He kept looking all over the place like he was a secret agent or something. I was like, "Dude chill out! It's just an I-pod!" Some people are like that though, just tell yourself, "I am not one of those people!" and you will be just fine!

Well, now that we've gotten all the drama bitcoin mama's out of the way. Let's figure out where we can meet to get these bitcoins. One of the best places to trade bitcoins is usually in a public place such as a coffee shop. Starbucks has always been a personal favorite of mine and of course is extremely convenient, since everyone Bitcoin trader should know what a Starbucks is, it's a good point of reference and there are about a gazillion to choose from in any given city.

But no matter where you go, just make sure that you are always surrounded by people in a well lit area. If you are conducting a larger transaction you may even be able to get permission from your local bank to conduct your trade in a conference room there. As bitcoins are rising to prominence many banks have agreed to participate in bitcoin exchanges.

The nature of the exchange usually allows for the person who posted the advertisement (The Seller) to be paid first. This is not necessarily set in stone but this is the usually method employed when it comes to bitcoin person to person exchange. First you pay them with some source of conventional currency such as U.S. dollars and then after that the seller can then transfer the agreed upon amount of bitcoins to your public address in your bitcoin wallet. Then, voila! Like magic you will receive your bitcoins in the wallet attached to your smart phone or lap top and the exchange is complete.

Another aspect of the exchange that you may want to employ, especially for larger transactions is that of using an escrow, relying upon multiple signatures for the transfer of bitcoins to be enacted, with a third party holding on to the money until the transaction has been completed.

One very special difference between the escrow that bitcoin transfer provides compared to that of a more traditional service is that unlike a traditional escrow that can refuse a return of funds, the multi signature based escrow used in Bitcoin transactions cannot hold onto the money, and if a transfer is not made it must return it. This is due to the fact that with multi signature escrow a third party at no time has full control of the money, the third party is simply a moderator that decides whether or not the funds will transfer between the buyer and seller.

Something that makes exchanges with Bitcoin unique among digital transactions is the fact that this currency once it is transferred that transfer is irreversible. It has been described as holding properties akin to loose cash. For example if someone just drops a million bucks out of a hot air balloon and people on the ground scoop it up, there is no feasible way to get that money back.

The same thing for bitcoins, once you send these coins out there is no binding legal authority to get them back. Bitcoins which use a transaction that relies on pure mathematics has know binding contract so just like the money thrown out of our hypothetical balloon once it floats away form us it is not retrievable. This property has led to bitcoins to be referred to as digital cash. Once that transaction is made, nothing you do or say can bring it back. This aspect of Bitcoin being irreversible is of great benefit to the sellers involved with Bitcoin. This way a payment for any product is guaranteed. Just like when someone sells a car and says that they

prefer, "cash only" the seller utilizing Bitcoin is guaranteed to get their payment since just like a cash only arrangement, bitcoin transactions are in fact irreversible. Being irreversible has great benefit in this regard.

Its very nature helps it as a trustworthy standard when traded between private individuals as well. Going to special Bitcoin trading groups such as "Square" and the "satoshi" group you can be introduced to many who are willing to trade their bitcoins in for cash. Some sites that might be useful to find these traders are,

"LocalBitcoin.com" and "TradeBitCoin.com".

E-bay can also be utilized as a trading resource but whatever you do, be sure to research the seller's feedback, a good or bad review should be enough to tell you whether or not you are confronted with a bad dealer. Along with all of these common security measures your prime instinct should tell you what to do and beyond anything else remember; it if it seems too good to be true, it probably is too good to be true.

5. What is Blockchain Technology?

In the traditional system of fiat money, governments are responsible for printing money as and when they need it. However, when it comes to Bitcoins, they cannot be printed. Bitcoins are discovered. Computers across the globe will mine for these Bitcoins by competing against one another. People keep making use of the Bitcoin network for sending Bitcoins to one another across the world.

Unless and until someone actually keeps a track of who is sending what to whom, no one will be aware of all these transactions. The Bitcoin network would deal with this all by collecting the data regarding all the transactions that were conducted during a set period into a list.

This list is referred to as a block. It is the job of the miner to confirm all such transactions and then write them in a ledger. This ledger comprises of a list of blocks and this list is referred to as the blockchain. This can be made use of for exploring any particular transaction that could have taken place between two Bitcoin addresses.

When a new list of transactions is created, it will be added on to the blockchain. It will, in turn, create a lengthy list of transactions that took place in the Bitcoin network. An updated copy of a block would be given to everyone who participates in it, so they will be aware of what is going on.

However, can you always trust this ledger and is all of this held in digital format? How do you make sure that this blockchain will stay intact and it is not tampered with? This is the point where the

"miners" come into the picture.

When a block of transactions has been created, then the miners will put it through a particular process. They will take the information that is present in a block and apply the mathematical formula or equation to it for turning it into something different. The result would be a shorter sequence of letters and numbers that seem random and this is referred to as a hash.

This hash would be stored in the block at the end of a blockchain. These hashes have got a couple of interesting properties. It is really easy to create a hash from all the data that is present in the blockchain. However, it is impossible to find out what the original data was by looking at the hash. It is easy to produce a hash from huge amounts of data; each hash is unique in itself. If you change even one character in the block of Bitcoin, then the hash will change too.

Miners not only make use of the transactions present in a block for generating the hash, they make use of other bits of data as well. One such piece of data would be the hash of the previous block of Bitcoin from the blockchain.

Since the hash of each block is produced by making use of the hash from the previous block in the blockchain, this forms a digital wax seal. This provides the confirmation that the particular block, and every other block after it is legal and it has not been tampered with. If it has been tampered with, then the others would know about it.

If you try and fake a transaction by changing the block that is stored within the blockchain, then the hash of that block would change as well. If someone were to check the legitimacy of the transactions in the blockchain by running it through the hashing equation, then the fake block will be spotted instantly. Since the hash of every block is made use of for producing the hash of the subsequent block in the chain, simply tampering with the hash of one would result in the subsequent hash going wrong as well.

This would continue until the very end of the chain and all the blocks will be tampered with.

6. The Good, Bad, and Ugly of Cryptocurrency

Cryptocurrency, or the electronically created line of codes of monetary value, or simply put, digital currency can be defined as a medium of exchange just like the usual currencies such as USD. However, what makes them different from the conventional currencies is that they are designed to exchange digital information by using the principles of cryptography. This cryptography controls the security of transactions as well as the mining of new coins.

Bitcoin was the first crypto-currency that was mined back in 2009. Since then, there have been several players like dogecoin, litecoin etc that are also referred to as the Altcoins.

The beauty of this form of currency is that they are not controlled by central banks like Federal Reserve System. It is fully decentralized and is in no way governed by the federal or government authorities. When compared to the traditionally mined currencies, digital ones cannot be monopolized, accelerated, stunted or abused by a group or an individual. The specified amount of currency is produced by a community as a whole and its rate is already defined as well as disclosed publically.

Cryptocurrency is digital, it is on the internet, it does not belong to one country and thus do not require a central bank. Its value is determined by the market demand and supply, by the user. The only flip side to this otherwise novel concept is its complete anonymity.

While it is treated as Bitcoin's ultimate USP, it has also opened up floodgates of potential abuse. Since it is untraceable, a niche for illegal transactions has been created inadvertently. There is no central repository, no law enforcement and the payment processors do not fall under any form of jurisdiction for their bitcoin accounts. The path of digital currency, popularly known as Bitcoin, is the one pockmarked with shoddy past.

Let us take a look at the several features of a Bitcoin that set it apart from fiat currencies.

The Bitcoin is decentralized. This means that one particular authority does not control it. Every machine that can mine Bitcoin and processes these transactions would become a part of this network. All the machines will work together. Theoretically, this means that one particular authority does not have the power to take away people's Bitcoin.

Even if a part of the network happens to go offline due to some reason, money will still keep on flowing in. All the conventional banks have got a multistage procedure for opening a bank account. Setting up the merchant accounts is another long and tiresome procedure. When it comes to Bitcoin, you can set up your Bitcoin address in no time and without the payment of any fees. It is kind of anonymous as well.

Users are allowed to have multiple Bitcoin addresses and these addresses aren't linked to any names, addresses, or any other personal information. The functioning of the Bitcoins is completely transparent. Every transaction that takes place is stored in the network in a ledger format and this is referred to as the blockchain. Blockchain says it all. If your Bitcoin address is public then anyone will be able to tell the number of Bitcoins that are stored at that address.

However, they wouldn't know to whom the address belongs. There are different measures that you can take for making your activities more protected on the Bitcoin network. Any bank would charge a transaction fee for any international transaction. However, the Bitcoin doesn't do so. You will also be able to transfer money anywhere in the world and the receiver would receive it within moments.

The Bitcoin network processes transactions rather quickly. Once you have sent Bitcoin out of your account, there is no way that you will get them back. If the recipient sends them back then you can get them. If not, they are gone forever.

7. The Bitcoin Boom

Bitcoin funds can then be used just like any other form of money to purchase whatever item the user desires to obtain. The value attached to various items through Bitcoin may be a bit confusing at first; depending on the method of calculation used some purchases require Bitcoin values that are in the decimal range. And if you hate math like me you may get a little anxious to see all those decimals poking up at you.

But not to worry, for the mathematically challenged like myself they have broke it down for us. They have greatly simplified the decimal notation and created simpler value markers such as the "satoshi". Taking its name right from the pseudonym of the founder, a Satoshi represents the smallest measurement in Bitcoin, "0.00000001; that is, one hundred millionth of a Bitcoin. So instead of choking down all of those decimals when making a bitcoin transaction, you can just say, "Hey Buddy! That bag of chips costs 199 Satoshi's!"

Without these easy demarcations things do get pretty blurry. I remember a couple of years ago trying to sell this dude a video game and the first thing he mentioned was to sell it to me in bitcoins. I didn't know a whole lot about it back then, but being the open minded adventurer that I am I gave it a go. Well, to make a long story short, this guy didn't say anything about Satoshi's! When I met up with him he kept rattling off stuff about paying me all kinds of numbers and decimal point values of bitcoins that didn't make much sense to me. If only he told me about the satoshi! It would have made so much sense!

The other two main values in Bitcoin are that of the millibitcoin (mBTC) and microbitcoin (uBC) The value of the microbitcoin is 0.000001 and for a millibitcoin it is 0.001. These values have been the standard bearers. These three modes of calculation have remained a steady standard but other aspects of Bitcoin's value have changed quite a bit over its six year history.

The first major milestone came on May 18, 2010 when a Bitcoin user exchanged 10,000 bitcoins to another user in exchange for two large pizzas. It sounds completely ridiculous now but this was among the first of small scale exchanges being made with the currency. At the time one Bitcoin was worth less than a penny making the users pizza purchase valued at a little less than ten dollars.

Then flash forward to 2014 and a Lamborghini that was worth over 200,000 U.S. dollars was purchased with just 216 bitcoins. This is just how drastic the rise in value of bitcoins has been. By February 9, 2011 when the bitcoin had reached parity with the U.S. dollar those two pizzas that had been purchased just a year before were suddenly worth 10,000 bucks. No one ever dreamed how rapid the ascendancy of the bitcoin would be and what had begun as a kind of joke and hobby for many bitcoin miners has become a very serious business. The reason why the value of Bitcoin is subject to such change is because of the fact that its value is based on that of its perceived

"store of value" as opposed to being set against "fiat currencies". Fiat currency is a currency that is based upon and gets its value from government regulations and laws. Bitcoin is a currency that is not tied down to any form of fiat.

A "fiat" currency is a national currency that is regulated by

governments, whereas a "store of value" currency is just like the name implies, a currency that is stored and can increase in value over time. This increase however depends upon how much of it is in circulation, so bitcoins store of value depends completely on how much is being traded at the time.

Bitcoin is currently worth $244.10. On average the exchange rate fluctuates from $0.01 to over $30 per BTC. This value is estimated to change in the not too distant future. It is the fact that bitcoins do not go through a centralized bank that is responsible for this fluctuation. Since there is so far, no printed currency for Bitcoin, there is no set relative value either. The value has had some definite peaks, one of the biggest happened in the year 2011 when Bitcoin went from .005USD to $18.60001USD. And then buy October of 2012 bitcoins had dropped once again down to a little over $12 dollars. These fluctuations have led some to claim that the value of bitcoins is quite volatile.

But this is the nature of bitcoins, since it is not a government backed fiat currency and it has no set standard the actual value of bitcoins fluctuate simply from the whim of supply and demand. This has led many to joke that bitcoins have a status more akin to a collector's item then an actual currency, because just like your old comic books and baseball cards on e-bay, the value fluctuates based on the supply and demand of the item or in this case bitcoin.

Just like that Superman comic book from 1939, bitcoins were designed to have a fixed amount that would be put in circulation. The number of bitcoins that will ever be mined and used is capped at 21 million. So just like that Superman comic book that has a limited supply in circulation, the law of supply and demand kicks in, and the fewer and fewer that are left in circulation the more the individual comic (or bitcoin) will be worth. With bitcoins tied to this law of supply and demand they are constantly in a state of deflation, meaning that their value is incessantly on the rise.

This is the opposite of inflation, which is the usual cause of crisis in government run currency. With many other monetary systems it was runaway inflation caused by the printing out of too much money that drastically reduced the value of that nation's money. Bitcoin however does not have that kind of problem since there is no way to print this currency out. So rather than inflation, bitcoins are in a state of deflation, their value then is much more likely to increase as the currency deflates.

While at first this may seem like an inherently good thing to have value exponentially increase. Economists (the nay sayers!) cite deflation as a potential downfall for bitcoins and some even bring up the doom and gloom of a deflationary spiral. Citing for example, among their many other concerns, the idea that as the value of bitcoins rise astronomically through the roof, so will our debt! This is long held standard of economists that too much deflation can spiral out of control and lead to these kinds of dire predicaments. That is a scary thought for the nation and any other individual consumer who may have experienced their own personal debt. The idea that your debt could increase in value is bizarre and frightening.

Just like the collector's item analogy, your debt could raise in its value. Well, in that case I don't want my student loans to become a collector's edition any time soon. I can hear them know yelling for it right now, "Step right up folks! Right here we have a pristine and mint condition Perkins Loan!"

Yeah, well, they can have that one! But jokes aside this is a dilemma that may have to be faced in the future, especially if bitcoins expand to take over much of the US dollars burdens, it will have to figure out what to do with the insurmountable levels of debt as well. Just what will happen if everything transfers over to Bitcoins? The solution for this one remains a bit unclear for the time being.

Bitcoin does however have an; albeit strange, but useful solution to one of the greatest arguments against deflation. Because among the concerns that have been tossed around in regard to the rising value of bitcoins is what will happen when the value of 1 bitcoin is so great it exceeds the worth of some of the more simple of products that you may want to buy.

In order to make this explanation a bit more understandable, for the sake of our example, let's switch away from the value of bitcoins and go back to our tried and true U.S. dollar. So instead of the bitcoin excessively deflating, let's imagine that the U.S. dollar is in deflation. Now let's pretend that this deflation of the U.S. dollar has raised the value of U.S currency so dramatically that the smallest unit of measure in USD, the penny, is now worth more than the value of a brand new car.

Well, the obvious question is, "How the heck do you buy that car?"

Do you just overpay and don't worry about the change? This is a situation where once and for all you can hand someone a penny and tell them, "Don't spend it all in one place!" and really mean it! Of course this is a fairly ridiculous example, but you get the idea. The penny is the smallest unit in U.S. currency; it can not go beyond that threshold. One cent simply won't divide any further.

Bitcoin however, does not have that problem. Since at its heart Bitcoin is a mathematical equation, you can divide it as much as you want. So if Bitcoin's value did continue to rise dramatically, unlike the penny, you can divide the bitcoin into smaller units of measure. In fact, this is already a common practice among bitcoin users. With bitcoins you can just keep moving the decimal place; right now the smallest known unit is at 0.00000001 and as mentioned earlier, in honor of its founder, is named a "Satoshi".

So if bitcoins were used in our car example, and you find that the car wasn't even worth one bitcoin, you can just subdivide until you have the right value to purchase the vehicle. So take that! Yes! In your face you economic haters! The bitcoin can survive! Sorry, just a little humor! I promise! I'm not that obsessed with bitcoins, but it is a very fascinating topic of debate nonetheless. And the rising value of bitcoins will be something very much worth our attention in the years to come.

8. The Future of Cryptocurrency

Now that we know beyond a shred of doubt that Bitcoin and BlockChain together are formidable, would you say that in coming years it will completely replace the traditional banking systems and would become the main source of transactions? So is there a future in digital currency or is it just another fad that will run its course in sometime? Let's have a look at some of the problems this currency is capable of solving:

- Bitcoins assure that at any given time, personal data is not compromised when the users transact. The privacy will always remain sacrosanct.

- Faultless transactions are possible by anyone using an internet connection. Simple internet availability will make banking facilities available even to the most remote areas.

- Petty transaction fee for international remittance when money is transferred using Bitcoins which is currently being charged at 10% by the banks

Even though Bitcoin does not have a centralized system, it hardly faces any threat because it is the user who determines the value of the digital currency. However, Bitcoin largely rests on the laurels of its base technology, BlockChain, which makes every transaction transparent. The potential of this technology far transcends beyond Bitcoin alone.

Even though BlockChain clearly star of the show, there are also many reasons that support the cause of the currency as much as the buzz around the technology. Bitcoin is essentially for the internet-savvy generation. You have the freedom to use it anywhere and anytime, for the least amount of fee. Since this currency cannot be duplicated, scams become less probable and the transactions become more secure, thanks to BlockChain, again! The identity of the user remains anonymous and is never revealed at any given point of time. You can create as many Bitcoin wallets as you like and not feel restricted by just single bank account operation.

The one thing that Bitcoin does best is to bring access of banking facilities to the unbanked. Many believe that it will make most practical sense in the developing countries where the infrastructure is in place but still the facilities have not yet been provided. For the unbanked population, the digital currency surely has a lot of potential and is also capable of solving many finance related problems for these people.

It is hard to say at this stage if Bitcoin will ever be big enough to overthrow the conventional monetary system but it does have a temporary appeal that seems quite convincing in the near future. The currency can take the power from the hands of the banks and place it in the hands of the customers for the first time and it is a safe speculation that the use and popularity of Bitcoin will definitely grow in the coming times. It has certainly made inroads in the financial sector and if they are able to secure and tighten their spot, Bitcoin will go places!

Different cryptocurrency wallet types Even though bitcoins are a digital currency, just like any other form of cash you are still going to need a wallet to store them in. Yes, money always needs to have that ever lovely accessory of alligator skin that you can fit snugly in your back pocket! You may be wondering though, "How the heck can I put a non-physical currency in a wallet?" Well my friend, the bitcoin wallet is an entirely different animal all together. Although I did once see a physical bitcoin wallet someone had as a bit of a gag, the wallets that we are talking about are of course a digital creation. Essentially the Bitcoin wallet is a collection of all of your private keys and addresses. The wallet is helpful to organize and group your bitcoins for their various purposes. You can allot a group of Bitcoins for a savings account, another for shopping and another on for bills. The wallet is completely customizable to your needs.

If you have an extremely large group of addresses built up your can further beef up your organizational skills by engaging in a Bitcoin wallet program, these programs are great for backing up private keys and also serves as a nice aid if you are new to the program because these programs offer additional help with sending your bitcoins out and creating new bitcoin addresses.

Bitcoin wallet programs lets user's to generate new Bitcoin addresses and send and receive their bitcoins as well as keeping track of how many bitcoins the user actually has to spend at any given time, this is done by scanning the block chain to detect whether bitcoins have been received at any of the addresses in the wallet. The main difference between any given wallet program is how it handles the above mentioned functions. The methodology may be different but the basic functions are the same in all Bitcoin wallet programs. But, as discussed in chapter 3, no matter what wallet program you use, every single one of them will need a private key to conduct their transactions. In the most basic arrangement private keys are simply found in the wallet of the user's device in the form of what is called a

"wallet.dat.file" It was in this fashion that most of the first Bitcoin wallet programs conducted their business. One of the first wallet programs called, "Bitcoin QT" was a big user of this kind of system. There are some major flaws that were discovered with this kind of wallet program though. The number one flaw that is quickly evident to any user is the dilemma of having all of your wallet information open to the internet. Since the private key stored in what is known as a "hot wallet" on a device connected to the internet, there is no one to ensure that a hacker cannot infiltrate your system. Using coming hacking tactics such as malware, Trojans and Key Loggers any hacker who gains remote access to your computer could easily get access to the keys stored on your device, leaving you with an empty wallet and a very bad feeling in the pit of your stomach.

Because of the prevalence of such attacks, a hot wallet that opens up your information to the internet can never be completely trusted.

Even with antivirus programs actively running and scouring your hard drive on a daily basis, there is still always the possibility that someone may be able to find some kind of crack in your protection and break through.

This is why for many the best solution has been to close the door in the hackers face all together by taking their information offline. Because of the constant threat of infiltration that a common internet connection opens for us, some of the best programs of protection involve a hybrid system of an online computer without keys and an offline computer with keys. Because if it is not online, then short of breaking into your house and stealing your hard drive, the cyber crooks cannot get to it.

One of the most surprising features of Bitcoin to those that are just starting out is the fact that you can generate new addresses while you are offline. I can hear you voicing your doubt now, "Generating things offline? Without the help of my Inter Webs? Impossible!" Oh but it is! Contrary to popular belief the internet is not needed for every action we take. As of 2015 we can still live and breathe without it. And along with being able to obtain oxygen without a router we can also generate Bitcoin addresses.

A wallet program is perfectly capable of spewing out a random sequence of numbers without an internet connection. This random sequence of numbers is of course your address. You can do whatever you want with this sequence once it is created. You can write it down and tape it under a desk, or some other good hiding spot, or if you have a good memory you can simply memorize the address, and that way leave no physical trace of the address at all. By way of memorization you would be essentially turning your own brain into the wallet that the address is stored in. For those that like to throw around technical terms, your brain has now become a "brain wallet" but that is just bitcoin jargon for, "I memorized some numbers!"

The fact that you can take control of your bitcoin address completely independent of an internet connection may come as a surprise but once you have a wallet program set up you can arrange to have multiple addresses created that never go online and therefore are never at risk of being compromised. In this hybrid system of using an online device and an offline device, no further communication with the network is needed and your address is then generated at random. Having keys that are produced offline in this fashion is known as "cold storage".

But don't get confused, when we say "cold storage" we don't mean tossing your keys into the refrigerator with your cold cuts! It is called cold storage simply due to the fact that there is not a "hot" connection to the internet available to the device that generated these private keys, so any bitcoins sent to that corresponding address are referred to be in cold storage. Bitcoins sent via a hot connection to the internet, utilizing an online device or computer are then said to be in "hot storage".

Being able to generate these private keys offline is a rather unique feature that surprises a lot of people. And of course you are probably wondering how in the world someone can send you bitcoins when you are not even online. You just have to keep in mind that when someone wants to transfer bitcoins to you all they need is the address. So even if you have an address in cold storage generated on an offline computer, if you give this public address (public not private!) to whomever wants to send you bitcoins, they can start slinging those bitcoins in your direction with ease!

So its as simple as e-mailing someone your public key (address) and they can start sending you bitcoins, and at the same time your private key remains completely confidential in cold storage on your offline computer or device that created it. This is a great way to do business, just keep in mind that even though you do not need to be online for new addresses to be generated you do have to be online to see any money or activity that has accrued on your account.

One of the most popular forms of having a wallet in cold storage is that of the "paper wallet". Believe it or not, as we have already discussed, just like the name implies, a paper wallet is as simple as that, a piece of paper that you use to write down your private key on.

Wow, that is low tech at its best! Pen and paper! What's next bitcoin rock and chisel wallets?

Low tech as it is though; these methods are sometimes the best way to combat would-be high tech cyber criminals. Just make sure that you keep your paper wallet in a place that is safe, such as a filing cabinet or a lock box. And in the rare chance that someone would find it and realize the significance of what it was, I would suggest trying to keep the actual contents of the key itself as vague as you possibly can. This is after all the very nature of cryptology. The goal is to make it as hard to decipher and extract data from as you possibly can.

And not to get too cryptic with my own cryptology but I have written private keys in the middle of grocery lists and old book of poetry I wrote. And now that I have revealed my secret to millions of people on the internet lets hope no cyber criminals crawl through my window searching for my grocery receipts! But that is how I handle paper keys, I just put them right smack dab in the middle of milk, bread, and love sonnets. That way I have a series of jumbled up letters and numbers that only I would get the gist of. I'd like to see the Davinci crack that code!

But that's just something that I have come up with. The standard tool of encrypting a paper wallet does not have you writing down the private key on a piece of paper at all. Instead of writing down the key itself you simply write down the encrypted version of it. After this has been achieved the only way to decrypt the private key is to do so with a password that you had chosen previously for it. Another interesting security feature that draws upon the idea of hybridization that was mentioned earlier merges aspects from both hot and cold wallets in the application of what has come to be termed "offline transaction signing". This method involves the use of two computers. One computer utilizes a personal hot wallet, everything is up and running on this hot wallet but the private keys have been purposefully omitted.

Having a hot wallet set up like this creates an extra authorization step when you try to send out bitcoins. When you click "send bitcoins" you will then be prompted to carry out a digital authorization from your other offline wallet. This is the part that you use a second offline computer or device that has a wallet installed and use it to digitally sign the authorization request of the first computer. You take this second computer and use it to create a file that has the digital signature of the transaction and then copy this signature to the online computer which will in turn send it out to the Bitcoin network.

The genius of this is that your online computer never gains access to the actual contents of the private keys. The digital signature does not contain any specific contents related to the keys themselves either; because all the signature is comprised of is a generic stamp that signifies that the wallet program it came from has authorization for use.

Just like when you go to the bank and some random financial administrator puts his stamp of approval on something. That's all that offline transaction signing is. Although it may seem a bit complicated to go back and forth between one online and one offline computer the benefit of this system is that there is never a transition from cold to hot storage. Your bitcoins can remain permanently secure in cold storage during all of the transactions.

A new breakthrough on this idea is that of the "Hardware Wallet".

The hardware wallet is also able to produce the same offline digital signature, but instead of doing this with an offline computer it is done with a hand held device that simply plugs into the computer that contains the hot wallet. This method is completely secure; the private keys stored in this hand held device remain in safely in cold storage during the entire time of the transaction.

Even if the online computer you plug it into is riddled with viruses, these viruses have no way to access the private keys in this device. Without any fear you can plug this thing in, and when you click,

"send bitcoins" on your online computer all you have to do is press a button on this hardware wallet/device and it uses the internally stored private keys to gain digital authorization of the transaction. This is a completely secure and convenient way to use your bitcoins the only real hazard is losing the device itself. So if you have one of these try to keep your eyes on it at all times so as not to lose it or have it stolen.

But now that we have examined the deep freeze of cold storage let us take a look at some "hot wallets". Running on a software program off of your own personal device, hot wallets do not require any third party service to run them. The part of maintaining a hot wallet that requires the most vigilance is the protection of your private key which is exposed to the internet every time you connect to do business.

Using a hot wallet may provide you with constant easy access but as easy as it is for you to access your bitcoins it may be just as easy for a cyber-criminal to ask them as well. The security level is so low for a hot wallet that, short of just handing someone your information, it is by far the most risky way to use a wallet.

Using a hot wallet you have to be constantly aware of the danger of hackers, and malware viruses that could be used to steal your information and money. And now that I have thoroughly scared you to death about using a hot wallet, allow me to give you this little bit of respite; although it poses a big risk, the odds of someone hacking into your hot wallet are rare and just like in real life, with a physical wallet, as long as you don't go around broadcasting all of your mullah and throwing bitcoins right in the face of a potential hacker you probably won't get hacked. But like winning the unlucky lottery, the risk is always there, and if you are unlucky enough to get targeted you and your bitcoins will be parted from each other very easily.

So if you do insist on using a hot wallet your best strategy is to keep as low a profile as possible. Your best deterrent is to stay unknown and off of the radar of any potential hackers. Never announce to anyone the amount of money you have and try not to keep too much cash in just one place. So be vigilant but don't have a heart attack!

Because it is a very unlucky lottery you would win, to have your whole bitcoin wallet ransacked by hackers. Just be smart about your transactions and at any sign of unusual activity take decisive action and you should be ok.

But for those of you who can not rest unless you know you have the best security that money and good intentions can buy, allow me to suggest the, "Armory" wallet. This wallet is touted as top of the line in security for a wide variety of reasons. Once you sign up for this wallet service you are given offline wallets with encryption so intense the Navajho code breakers couldn't have broke it!

9. Government vs. Bitcoin

By now, you're probably wondering who has the most amount of Bitcoin in the world. There are many people who own Bitcoin and there are a lot of people who have hundreds of thousands and millions of dollars worth of Bitcoin. These are mostly people who started in the game early and who grew their Bitcoin profits from the simple .0001 cents that each Bitcoin was originally worth.
What you may be surprised to find out is that not a single one of those people are actually the biggest Bitcoin holder in the world. In fact, the chances are that you would never even guess who the biggest owner of Bitcoin in the world is. Don't worry, though, you'll know by the end of the chapter after we finish discussing how Bitcoin and the United States government fit together.

Government Regulation
There is currently no regulation of Bitcoin from the United States government or any government. This is because Bitcoin is a fairly new concept and it is designed to work more like something that people own instead of something that people use as a way to pay for things.
There is always a chance that the government will begin to regulate Bitcoin but it generally takes over a decade to regulate different forms of currency. In the past, it took a long time to make the switch and then the government was not able to regulate two different types of currency so they had to choose one. The chances of Bitcoin being chosen are very slim.
When the government makes the decision to regulate Bitcoin, they will need to figure out how they are going to make it less anonymous and they will have to make sure that they are prepared for the pushback that will come from the people who currently own Bitcoin. It is a product that can be traded, not something that can be spent.

Not Currency
The United States government currently works hard to make sure that it is clear that Bitcoin is not actual currency. It is simply

something that people can use to trade for different things. They may pay money to be able to have it but, to the government, this is no different than paying money to buy stocks in a company or to buy into something that is just an idea.

There are some small regulations that come along with this type of trade and with people being able to buy into Bitcoin but it is nothing compared to the type of regulations that come along with currency. The government has very little control over what people are able to do with Bitcoin, how much they are able to be worth and how much different Bitcoin sellers are able to charge for the Bitcoin that people are buying from them.

In fact, it is such an unregulated type of trading that some conservatives think of Bitcoin as the black market.

Since it's not actually illegal and is on the up and up with the stock market, there is no way that Bitcoin is black market.

Owners of Bitcoin

In the past, people who owned a lot of Bitcoin were monitored by the government very closely. This was something that came along with those same people being watched for silk-road related purposes. The majority of people who had a lot of Bitcoin in one wallet were the ones who were not doing things that were legal and who were participating on the Silk Road.

Many people who own Bitcoin know better, though. They know that they should keep their Bitcoin in different wallets. Because of this, it appears that many more people own Bitcoin than what was originally thought. This is especially true of the people who have had Bitcoin since it first started. Each one has multiple wallets that they work from so it is nearly impossible to judge how much Bitcoin each of the people has.

This also makes it more difficult to track them, contributing even further to the idea that Bitcoin is focused on the anonymity of the people who use it and that it is something that anyone with an email address and a bank account is able to access without having to give up the specific details of their identity.

Problems from Government

The biggest problem that comes for Bitcoin is from the government aspect of it. The problem is because the government does not regulate it and they currently have no way to do so. Because of this, they look down on the use of Bitcoin. The government has no say-so in how Bitcoin is handled, what it can be used for and the way that it is able to be sold. Because of this, the government has worked hard to shut down the operations of Bitcoin.

In 2015, when the Silk Road was seized, they actually thought that they had shut down Bitcoin. They found a lot of Bitcoin during that time and they believed that it was all of the Bitcoin in the world.

What they didn't know, though, was that Bitcoin was used in other areas aside from the Silk Road. Bitcoin still existed even after the Silk Road shut down.

Shut Down of the Silk Road

As 2015 came to a close and the trials began for the Silk Road, the FBI found that they had a problem on their hand: Bitcoin. It wasn't necessarily illegal to have like some of the other digital property that the people who were on the Silk Road owned but it was somewhat of a conundrum for the people who seized all of the things that came off of the Silk Road.

The FBI had no idea what to do with it.

As they continued to work on the Silk Road and seize different things from it, they took more and more from the biggest players on the Silk Road. They worked to make sure that they had everything that the people who had worked on the Silk Road had and they did everything that they could to make sure that there was nothing left. This included the seizure of the Bitcoin that people had paid in on the Silk Road.

The FBI is the biggest owner of Bitcoin thanks to the seizure of the Silk Road. Since Bitcoin seemed like property and really had no official classification, the FBI seized them as if they were property. The FBI currently holds 144,000 Bitcoin. That number is worth over 100 thousand American Dollars.

*Note: while the FBI is the official owner of the largest collection of Bitcoin, the chances that someone else has an even larger collection are high. Since so many people who use Bitcoin choose to keep it in separate wallets, it is impossible to tell how many wallets are assigned to each person. One person could have 30 wallets that each have 20 thousand Bitcoin in them. Because of this, there is reason to believe that the creator of Bitcoin, whose official identity has never been revealed, has the largest collection and has over 50 wallets that the Bitcoin are all stored in.

10. Benefits of Cryptocurrency

The strength of the cryptocurrency lies in its simplicity of being able to transact, the lack of middlemen, and has no government interference. Over the last few years, cryptocurrency has been gaining a lot of property. In the initial phase, it seemed as scary as the credit card did to its users in the initial days of credit cards becoming available. You might have heard terms like Bitcoin or ether.

These are types of cryptocurrencies that make use of block chain technology for keeping it safe and secure. At present, there are different types of cryptocurrencies that are available and a quick Google search will tell you all about it. Once the cryptocurrency becomes stable, there would be little scope for either inflation or deflation. In this chapter, let us look at the different benefits that cryptocurrency has to offer.

Scam

Cryptocurrencies are digital in nature and they cannot be forged. Not just that, they cannot be reversed arbitrarily by the sender just like the charge backs on the credit card.

Instant settlement

Purchasing real property involves a few third parties (like lawyers or notary), delays, and also the payment of a fee. Bitcoin or cryptocurrency can be thought of as a large database of property rights. Bitcoin contracts can be designed and then enforced to either eliminate or add the approvals of a third party, any reference to external facts, or it should be completed at a date in the future for a fraction of the expense and the time that is required for the completion of the traditional asset transfer.

Lower fees

There is no transaction fee that is levied on cryptocurrency exchange since the miners are already compensated by the network. Even though there is no transaction fee, most would expect that the users would make use of a third party service like Coinbase for the creation and the maintenance of their Bitcoin folders.

These services are similar to PayPal and provide the online exchange system for Bitcoins and are likely to charge a user fee. PayPal neither accepts nor transfers Bitcoins.

Identity theft

When you give your credit card to a vendor or a merchant, then you will be giving them access to your credit line, regardless of the quantum of the transaction. Credit cards usually operate on what is referred to as pull basis. This means that once the store has initiated the payment, then the assigned amount would be automatically pulled from your concerned account.

Cryptocurrency, on the other hand, makes use of a push technique. This would mean that the holder of the cryptocurrency could send exactly the amount that the holder would want to give to the merchant.

Access to everyone

There are more than 2.2 billion people out there who have got access to the Internet or even mobile phones but don't have access to the traditional exchange. Such people are the ones that are suited for cryptocurrency. M-PESA is a mobile-based service that helps in transferring money and also in micro financing.

This service has also announced a Bitcoin device and now one in every three Kenyans has got a Bitcoin wallet.

Decentralization

A huge network of computers all over the world makes use of blockchain technology for managing the Bitcoin database and the transactions. A network, not a single authority, controls Bitcoin. Decentralization in here would signify that the network would operate on a peer-to-peer basis or a user-to-user basis. This helps in forming collaboration instead of a controlling authority.

Universal recognition

Cryptocurrencies aren't bound by exchange or interest rates; they

don't have any transaction fees or any other charges applicable in any country. This makes them suitable for international usage without having to face any problems.

This will in turn help in saving time and money for conducting business, instead of having to spend hours, for transferring money from one country to another. It can operate at an international level and can be used with ease.

There isn't an electronic cash system that you can make use of

wherein your account wouldn't be owned by a third party. For instance, take the example of PayPal. If the company has decided that your account has been or is being misused for any reason, then it has got the power to freeze all of your assets without having to consult you.

It is then your responsibility to get it all cleared up for regaining access to your funds. When you use cryptocurrency, you will have a private key that would have a corresponding public key that would make up the address of your cryptocurrency. This cannot be taken away from you unless you lose it on your own.

Cryptocurrency has got a long road ahead of itself before it is capable of replacing traditional forms of currency and credit cards before being accepted as the global commerce tool.

Most people are still unaware of how cryptocurrency works or what cryptocurrency is. They will need to be educated about all this before they can apply it. Businesses will have to start accepting it and they will need to make it simpler for signing up and getting started with this.

Cryptocurrency will help you have complete control over your money and it is quite secure. When made use of in a proper manner, it will be a force to be reckoned with. It will definitely change the global commerce map.

11. Conclusion

Tips and Fun Facts About Bitcoin

Bitcoin is clearly a great way to make money and is something that is a technological revolution. It was created for simple purposes but it has grown into so much more. Because of the way that people are able to use Bitcoin, there are a few things that you should look for when you are shopping for Bitcoin and when you are using Bitcoin in different instances.

The Lowest Price

Always look for the lowest price possible when it comes to Bitcoin and buying it. Keep track of the prices and get predictions for what the price is going to be like. While there is no way to be certain how far the price is going to go up (or down), you can do certain things to make sure that you are watching the patterns. This will give you a great chance at being able to get the lowest price and to always make sure that it is going to be the best investment for you.

If you see that Bitcoin is at the lowest price throughout the day, you should take the time and buy it at that point. The chances are that it will go back up and you will not be able to get that same price again so that you will need to make sure that you are going to get more out of the Bitcoin and that you will not have to make as big of an investment in the Bitcoin that you have.

Getting Bitcoin for the lowest price possible is a key part of making sure that you can truly get a good return on your investment.

The Highest Price

The highest price will always be the best price for you to make sure that you are getting a good return on your investment.

If you find that you are not going to be able to sell it for what you paid for, wait until you are able to sell it for that price or more. The people who waited out the time periods where Bitcoin was taking huge drops in price were then able to make up for it when it went back up as the idea behind the cryptocurrency was just getting started. You should do the same.

Fastest Growing
Bitcoins were the fastest growing investment introduced in the new millennium. This is because they went from being worth $0 to being worth over $1,000 in just seven years. The Bitcoin industry went from nothing to booming during that time and people were able to make a lot of the money back that they initially put into Bitcoins.

It has been declared as the fastest growing investment and predictions put it at having unlimited growth potential. Eventually, a single Bitcoin could be worth into the millions.

Competitors
There have been so many competitors of the Bitcoin that they had to start coming up with a name to group them all together. While Bitcoin was the first to coin the term cryptocurrency, it is now used for Bitcoin and the competitors that it has.

While there are competitors on the market that are trying to become as big as Bitcoin, not a single one of them has been able to see even a fraction of the growth that Bitcoin has seen.

Other forms of cryptocurrency include things like "Lite Coins" and Ethereum. None of them have really been able to compete with Bitcoin because of the market that Bitcoin now dominates and because of the way that the system is set up to ensure that Bitcoin is going to be the biggest and best option on the market.

There can be cryptocurrency and they can try to compete with Bitcoin but, unless there is a huge shift in the market, there won't ever be another Bitcoin.

No Replication

Unlike real money, there is no way to replicate Bitcoin. This involves the coding process that comes around when Bitcoin are created. Since they all have a unique code that is attached to them, it would be impossible for anyone to make a copy of a Bitcoin.

This is one thing that is especially promising for banks and other financial professionals. With Bitcoin, there is no way to make counterfeit. Despite all of the technology (or, perhaps, because of all of it), there is still a huge problem with counterfeit money throughout the world. Bitcoin eliminates all of that.

Bitcoin Cash
In 2016, Vancouver in Canada became the first state to officially have an ATM where you could get cash for your Bitcoin. Just like the selling model that is online, you will need to pay a fee to be able to get that cash but it adds an extra level of convenience for people who have Bitcoin and who want to be able to get the cold, hard cash for the Bitcoin that they have worked so hard to collect.

Expect to pay slightly more than the normal selling fee that you would find on a site if you want to be able to cash out your Bitcoin using an ATM-style machine.

Buying Cars

If you want to buy a car from an individual seller, you might be able to pay in Bitcoin. The availability of Bitcoin for cars and things similar really depends on the person who is selling it and if they are selling it in an individualized format. There were no big dealerships or car brands that offered buyers the chance to buy cars in Bitcoin until one company stepped up and decided that they could make some extra money by allowing people to buy their cars with Bitcoin. This company was none other than luxury genius car company, Lamborghini. They now accept Bitcoin at every one of their dealerships across the United States and in other countries. You can also pay on their website with your Bitcoin if you are creating a completely customized version of your dream car. When you pay with Bitcoin at Lamborghini, you can also expect to be able to pay for all of your services that they perform. Oil changes, car washes, and services can all be paid for with Bitcoin at Lamborghini dealerships.

Ban on Bitcoin

There is no place in the world that has an official ban on Bitcoin in the traditional sense. You will not go to jail for getting caught with Bitcoin but banks in China could face serious problems if they allow the trade of Bitcoin to happen at the bank.

It is important to note that China created a ban on Bitcoin training for banks. Individuals are still allowed to trade Bitcoin for the time being and they will continue to be allowed to do so if there are no problems with Bitcoin.

Banks in China face charges, fines, and possible closures if they allow Bitcoin trading within the bank. The reasoning for this is China feels that Bitcoin is more of a currency than a trading item.

They want to make sure that people are not trading "money" through the bank and that everyone is being treated fairly when it comes to their opportunity to trade Bitcoin.

China simply does not want banks to take up all of the positive parts of Bitcoin and take them away from people who have sold them.

New Bitcoin

Whether you are interested in mining or not, it may be the way to go if you are looking for a fortune in Bitcoin. Each day that there is Bitcoin mining going on, there are 3,600 new Bitcoins created. That is the equivalent of nearly $400,000 – just shy of half of a million.

While you should know that you won't be able to find all the Bitcoins in one day while you are mining, it is something that is worth looking into for the Bitcoin fortune that you want to amass.

www.ingramcontent.com/pod-product-compliance
Lightning Source LLC
La Vergne TN
LVHW042352060326
832902LV00006B/552